THE CREATIVE ART OF

Decorative
Painting

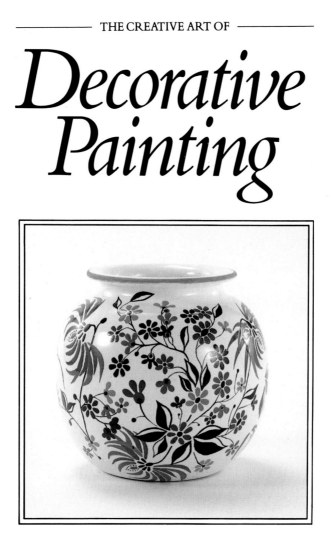

THE CREATIVE ART OF

Decorative Painting

Juliet Bawden

Longmeadow Press

The Creative Art of Decorative Painting

This 1989 edition published by
Longmeadow Press,
201 High Ridge Road,
Stamford, CT 06904.

ISBN 0-681-40725-5

© Salamander Books Ltd. 1988
52 Bedford Row,
London WC1R 4LR,
United Kingdom.

CREDITS

Editor-in-chief: Jilly Glassborow

Editor: Coral Walker

Designer: Kathy Gummer

Photographer: Steve Tanner

Line artwork: Malcolm Porter

Typeset by: The Old Mill, London

Color separation by: Fotographics Ltd, London – Hong Kong

Printed in Italy

CONTENTS

——— INTRODUCTION ———

With the vast new range of craft paints now available, it is easier than ever to create beautiful effects in the home. Sponged walls, stencilled tiles, spattered vases, personalized kitchen accessories and hand-painted china all help to reflect your own personality and add colour and style to your surroundings. And you don't have to be a highly skilled artist to achieve stunning results — many of the designs featured in this book rely on technique rather than the painter's ability to draw free-hand. Such techniques include sponging, masking, marbling, stencilling, stippling, ragging, bambooing and potato-cut printing.

There is something here to suit every taste and every level of dexterity, from easy projects for the less confident amongst you to complex designs for the more experienced. Each item is accompanied by colourful step-by-step photographs and easy-to-follow instructions on how to make it, and most of the projects can be done in an evening or a weekend. Where possible, templates have been provided at the back of the book for shapes that might prove difficult to copy free-hand.

Don't feel you have to follow each design slavishly. You may find an idea that interests you but you don't like the style or colour scheme in which it's been done; try experimenting a little and very soon you'll be creating your own imaginative designs.

— DECORATIVE PAINTING —

I n recent years, the growing interest in crafts and the shorter working week has meant that more and more people are trying their hands at new hobbies. In response to the increased demand for craft materials, manufacturers have been producing an increasingly wide range of products, and none more so than paint manufacturers. The result is that, whereas in the past decorative crafts such as fabric painting required a high degree of skill and a lot of expensive equipment, today, thanks to the vast new range of colourful, easy-to-use products, such hobbies are far more accessible and attractive to the general public.

In fact, the problem today tends to be more one of trying to make sense of the confusing array of different paint products available than of understanding how to use them. As you will find when using this book, the range of craft paints is now considerable, including glass paints, ceramic paints, acrylic paints, fabric paints, silk paints, stencil paints and crayons, leather dyes and multi-purpose felt tip paint pens. And, of course, you can also use traditional household decorating paints such as emulsions, eggshells and glosses, which come in a wide range of attractive colours, to create stunning effects on walls and furniture.

— WHAT TO PAINT —

One of the advantages of pursuing decorative painting as a hobby is that it enables you to create your own unique style in the home rather than having to conform to a prevalent trend, as you do when buying manufactured designs. And when it comes to deciding what to paint the choice is almost limitless. The photograph opposite shows a number of the items in this book before they were transformed. Ceramic plates, tiles and vases, glass tumblers and wine glasses, wooden boxes and frames, lampshades and oven gloves all look very dull in comparison to the colourful designs featured in later pages.

Some of the wooden items in this book are specially designed for painting and decorating, and are available from specialist craft suppliers (see craft magazines for stockists). Such items include the wooden boxes on pages 52/53 and 65, the clock on page 50, and the plant stand on pages 112/113. Other objects include old pieces of furniture that have been stripped down and given a new lease of life with an imaginative paint finish. Fabrics too can be painted to give a wide range of effects; either buy plain fabrics to make up into curtains, cushions or clothes, or buy ready-made items such as scarves, tee shirts, ties or even boxer shorts to decorate.

Plain items such as these are ideal for decorating, and there are paints available to suit any surface, be it wood, glass, ceramic, fabric or plastic.

—————————PAINT TECHNIQUES—————————

Having decided what to paint, you then have to decide how to paint it. Once again, the choice is extensive and includes techniques such as sponging (see pages 84, 93 and 104/105), stippling (page 83), ragging (pages 66 and 85), and marbling which can be achieved in one of two ways — either by floating oil or ceramic paints on water and putting the surface to be marbled in contact with the paints (see pages 23 and 64) or by hand-painting the design using a special glaze (pages 112/113).

Other techniques used in this book include masking (pages 25 and 106/107), potato-cut printing (page 70), transfer printing (page 79), bambooing (page 111) and stencilling (pages 32/33, 65, and 88/89). To make your own stencil you will need a cutting board, a stencil or craft knife, a sheet of acetate (special stencil acetate is available from craft shops) and your design. You will require a separate stencil for each colour being used. Tape a piece of acetate over your design and, using a permanent marker, trace that part of the design which is to be painted in the first colour. Trace the remainder of the design with a dotted line. Make a second and if necessary third stencil for subsequent colours. Now simply cut out the continuous line on each of the stencils using a stencil knife. Hold the knife as you would a pen and use the tip of the blade. Cut towards you, turning the stencil rather than the knife, and try not to lift the knife until you have completed a cut-out area. On a repeating stencil pattern, such as for a border, always draw a small part of the pattern either side of your main cut-out design so that you can use this for repositioning the stencil each time you finish painting a section.

DESIGN INSPIRATION

To begin with, you will probably want to follow the designs featured in this book (for which templates of the more complex ones can be found on pages 114-122). But as you become more confident and adventurous, you will no doubt start to look around for other ideas to copy or adapt. Many people believe that copying is cheating, but even the greatest designers of this and past ages would admit that they seek inspiration for their work from a wide range of sources. The photograph opposite shows you some of the many items to which you can turn for inspiration. Museums and art galleries can also provide an endless source of ideas.

Once you have worked out your design or found one to copy, you may find that it is too small (or too large) for your purposes. The easiest way to draw it to the size you need is to use a method known as squaring up. (This is the same method you will need to employ when using the templates at the back of the book.) First of all, trace your design on to a grid, using either graph paper or a grid drawn by hand; squares of 10mm (½in) should be suitable for this stage. Now draw a second grid on to tracing paper, making the squares either larger or smaller than the original grid, depending on what size you want your final design; for example, if the image is to be twice the size, make each square twice as large. Finally, copy the design, one square at a time, on to the new grid, being careful to note where the design enters and leaves each square.

If you have traced or squared up an image and you wish to transfer it to the object to be decorated, you can follow this simple procedure: turn your trace over and go over the outline on the reverse side with a soft pencil; now position the trace reverse side down on to the object and go over the outline once more. Alternatively, you can place a piece of carbon copy paper face down on to the surface of the object; place the design on top and draw round the outline.

Old china plates, ceramic tiles, books, magazines, postcards, fabrics and attractive packaging can all prove a source of inspiration for designs.

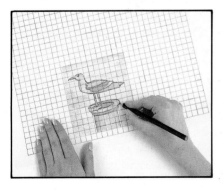

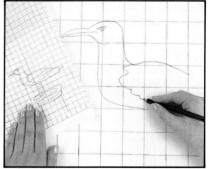

A simple way to change the size of a design is to square it up. Draw a grid on to tracing paper and trace an image of the design on to it.

Draw a second grid of larger squares (e.g. double the square size for an image twice as large) and copy the design, square by square, on to it.

DECORATIVE PRODUCTS

Today, a vast range of paints, pens, crayons and varnishes is readily available from craft shops and good department stores. Although, on the whole, the various products are intended for use on specific surfaces, you will find that some paints work well on more than one surface; for example, ceramic paints are suitable for use on glass, metal and wood, as well as china. Always try to use good quality brushes with these products and clean them immediately after use. Brushes used with solvent-based paints should be cleaned in white spirit or turpentine substitute; those used with water-based paints can be washed in water.

GLASS PAINTS

The glass paints used in this book are solvent-based paints that, on glass, give a stained glass effect; used on china and pottery they give a translucent finish. They are thick, sticky paints which require some practice to apply correctly, and they should always be used and left to dry (for at least 24 hours) in a relatively dust-free environment. The item to be decorated must be totally free from grease or dust before you begin. If necessary, wash the surface with warm soapy water, rinse and dry it, then wipe it with a cloth soaked in petroleum essence or methylated spirits. Apply the paint with a good quality, soft, clean, sable brush, well loaded with paint. The paint should be allowed to flow off the brush without leaving any brush strokes. A second coat may be necessary once the first has dried, in order to achieve a strong enough colour. Glass paints are also available in a water-based form.

Glass paints can be used in conjunction with a lead relief outline, which is applied straight from the tube, to give the effect of lead in a stained glass window. The paints are not suitable for objects that receive heavy wear, being most suited to purely decorative items. Objects should be washed in lukewarm soapy water.

CERAMIC PAINTS

Ceramic paints are solvent-based paints designed for use on clay and pottery, though they are also suitable for glass, metal and wood. They come in a wide range of colours and give a glossy, opaque finish. Ideally, they should be used on decorative objects or items which receive little wear. Avoid using cutlery on a painted surface as this will scratch the design, and never put decorated objects in a dishwasher; use warm soapy water to clean them. Ceramic paints require at least 24 hours to dry, after which you can apply a coat of ceramic varnish to help protect the design.

The wide range of craft paints now available includes glass paints, ceramic paints, fabric paints, special silk paints, stencil paints and crayons, and multi-purpose felt tip paint pens. You will require some good artist's brushes and, according to your needs, some stencilling and stippling brushes, a craft knife, masking tape, stencil acetate, low tack masking peel, a natural sponge and some varnish.

ACRYLIC PAINTS

Wooden objects such as doors and skirting boards are usually painted with oil-based gloss paints but, for smaller wooden items, water-based acrylic paints are far more suitable: they are easy to use, come in a wide range of bright colours, and dry very fast to give a rich glossy finish. Unlike gloss paints, you don't have to prepare the surface with primer and undercoat before applying acrylic paints; they can be painted straight on to bare wood. The paints are fully waterproof and are suitable for use both indoors and outdoors. They can also be used for painting designs on walls (see page 87). One word of warning though: be sure to clean your brush in water immediately after use, otherwise the paint will soon dry hard and ruin the brush.

There are various kinds of fabric paints available. Most need to be used on unbleached white or naturally coloured fabrics for the colours to remain true, but there are also paints available which are suitable for use on dark fabrics — these 'opaque' paints sit on top of the fabric as opposed to being absorbed into it. Fabric felt tip pens are very easy to use, but always remember to tape the fabric down before you begin to prevent it moving around. Transfer paints (see page 79) are for use on synthetic fabrics, though natural fabrics can be used if they are specially treated first.

Silk paints can be used on wool as well as silk. In this book they have been used in conjunction with coloured gutta, a gum-like substance which outlines each colour like lead outlines stained glass. (Clear gutta is also available; this is removed after the design is complete.) Before you begin to paint your silk, you must stretch the fabric across a silk or batik frame. The frames are available from craft shops and can be assembled to fit any size. Using special silk pins, begin to stretch your silk across the frame, starting in the middle of one side and pinning it down first to the left, then to the right. Do the opposite side in the same way, and complete with the remaining two sides. Draw the design on to the silk in gutta, using a special applicator bottle. Be sure to make the lines continuous — any gaps will allow the colour to seep through. Leave the gutta to dry for one hour before painting. (See pages 60 and 80/81 for designs.)

Once a design has been completed, fabric paints must be 'fixed' so that the colours do not run when the fabric is washed. Manufacturers will recommend the method best suited for fixing their products; such methods include heat or chemical treatments (see illustrations below).

Some fabric paints, such as these pearlized paints, can be fixed by heating the fabric for a few minutes with a hair dryer.

Most fabric paints, including fabric felt tip pens and certain silk paints, can be fixed by ironing on the reverse of the design.

OTHER PAINT PRODUCTS

Other products used in this book include multi-purpose felt tip paint pens that are suitable for use on almost any surface — china, glass, wood, leather, plastic etc. The pens are easy to use, fast drying and come in a wide range of colours. They are solvent-based and their strong smell can prove slightly overpowering, so you are advised to use them in a well ventilated room.

For stencilling paper and wood you can either use water-based stencil paints or oil-based wax stencil crayons. China items, such as the stencilled tiles and mugs on pages 20/21 and 32/33, can be painted with ceramic paints. Always use a special stencilling brush and apply the colour to the stencil cut-out using a circular motion. Begin at the edges and work inwards until the area is painted to your satisfaction. You can apply other colours on top of the first to provide shading and texture, but always change brushes between coats to avoid the colours becoming muddy.

VARNISHES

A coat of varnish will help to protect your paintwork. Polyurethane varnish is ideal for wood and comes in a matt or gloss finish. Ceramic varnish is specially designed for use on china and pottery. Other varnishes used in this book include patina and crackle varnishes. The former can be used to build up a high gloss, lacquer-effect finish on wood (see pages 52/53). Crackle varnish is applied over patina varnish that is not quite dry (see page 42). The difference in drying rates of the two varnishes causes the crackle varnish to craze, giving an 'antique' effect.

Some silk paints must be fixed in a special solution for five minutes, 48 hours after you have finished painting your design.

Ceramic paints are not very hard wearing so it is best to protect your design with a coat of ceramic varnish once the paints are dry.

–TABLE AND KITCHENWARE –

This chapter includes the use of ceramic, glass, fabric and acrylic paints. There are many different techniques covered, from masking and marbling to stencilling and free-hand painting. Styles range from the sophisticated and modern Torn Tape Plate on page 25 to the pretty and traditional napkin ring on page 39.

Items decorated with ceramic or glass paints should be handled with care and a coat of varnish is recommended to help protect the design. The paints are most suitable for use on purely decorative objects or items that are rarely used. Avoid using such items with cutlery and under no circumstances put them in a dishwasher.

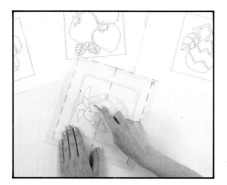

Here's an attractive way to brighten your kitchen — by stencilling your own tiles. Either square up the designs provided in the back of the book (as described on page 14) or draw your own design on to tracing paper. Using masking tape, attach the design to a cutting board. Tape the stencil film on top of the design and cut it out using a stencil knife.

Before your begin painting, wash and dry the tiles to make sure they are free from dirt and grease. Attach the cut stencil to a tile with masking tape. Pour some ceramic paint on to a saucer and dip the stencil brush into it. Dab off any surplus paint on to waste paper, then apply the colour to the required area of the stencil. Start with the lightest colour, then apply the darker tones on top.

Add subsequent colours to other areas of the stencil, again starting with the lightest and building up texture and shade with each application. Wait for the paint to dry before removing the stencil. Then carefully clean up any smudged areas with a craft knife or a paint brush dipped in turpentine. Finally, protect the design with a coat of ceramic varnish.

A very easy way of painting tiles is to use multi-purpose felt tip paint pens. Assuming each square represents one tile, square up your design (as described on page 14) and transfer it on to the tiles using a chinagraph pencil. Draw over this line with a fine line felt tip paint pen. Try to keep the paint flowing once you have put the pen on to the tile so that the line is continuous.

Colour in your design using both thick and fine line pens. Be as outrageous as you like with your use of colours, placing reds, oranges, and pinks together, and adding a sparkle with gold and silver.

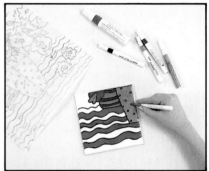

Add to the range of tones and colours with plenty of dots and lines in contrasting colours. To finish, protect your design with a coat of ceramic varnish once the paints are dry.

MARVELLOUS MARBLING

This must be the easiest way of achieving a stylish effect. All you need are some plain white tiles, ceramic or glass paints, white spirit, a large bowl full of water, a small mixing bowl or saucer and a paint brush. You may also wish to wear rubber gloves to protect your hands. Thin some paint with white spirit and begin to drop it on to the surface of the water with a paint brush.

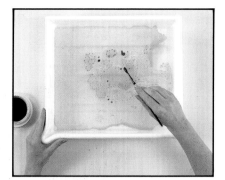

Using the handle of the paint brush or an old stick, mix the colour round so that it creates a swirling pattern. If you wish, you can dilute a second colour in the same way and add this to the first.

Carefully hold the glazed side of the tile against the surface of the water and then quickly lift it away. The tile will pick up the swirls of paint to give a marbled effect. Leave the tile to dry then give it a coat of ceramic varnish to protect the finish. You may find it necessary to practise this technique for a while before you perfect it.

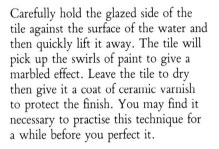

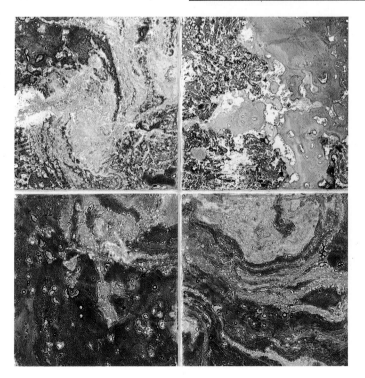

Transform a rather plain ceramic honey pot into something striking! Using a fine paint brush and black ceramic paint, paint some bees on to the lid of the pot. If you are worried about painting free-hand, first draw the bees on with a chinagraph pencil. And if you are not even sure how to draw a bee, get a picture of one to copy.

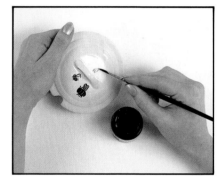

Now paint the stripes with black ceramic paint. If, like this one, your pot is ridged, use the raised surface as a guide for your lines of paint. Otherwise you can use strips of masking tape to mask off those areas which are to be yellow. In order not to smudge the work, you may find it easier to paint the lower half first and then leave it to dry before painting the top half.

When all the black has dried, apply the yellow ceramic paint, carefully filling in the bee's striped body with a fine brush. Fill the pot with honey and have a nice breakfast!

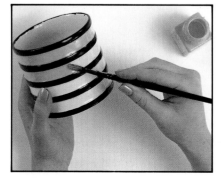

Create a stunning design by using a very simple but effective design technique, known as masking. Cut a strip of masking tape the width of your plate and very carefully rip it in half lengthways, creating an uneven edge. Place the two torn pieces back to back across the centre of the plate. Then add further double strips of tape either side, leaving gaps in between each set.

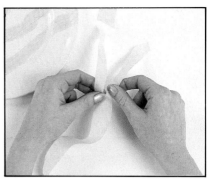

When you have covered the plate in torn tape lines, make sure that all the edges are stuck down properly. Apply ceramic paint to the exposed areas, using a dabbing motion so that the paint does not seep under the tape.

Leave the plate to dry for at least 24 hours before carefully removing the tape. Clean up any smudged edges using a rag dipped in white spirit, then apply a coat of ceramic varnish. The black lines on a white background gives a striking 'zebra stripe' effect, but other colour combinations look equally attractive so try experimenting a little.

Clowns are a very bright and jolly popular image and, painted on to wall plates like these, they make a colourful decoration for a child's room. Look at birthday cards, wrapping paper, toys and in children's books for inspiration.

Once you have drawn your design on paper, copy it on to a plate using a chinagraph pencil. When drawing your design, consider the shape of the plate; make the feet curl round the edge, as we have done here, and try to make the image fill as much of the plate as possible. Next, follow the chinagraph line with a line of black ceramic paint.

Colour the main features such as clothes and hair using very bright ceramic paints: cherry red, lavender, blue, orange, yellow and green. Make the clothes colourful and busy, with plenty of spots, checks and patches.

Finally, fill in the background with circles, triangles or wavy lines, painted in brightly contrasting colours. When the paint has dried, finish off with a protective coat of ceramic varnish.

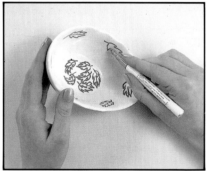

Brighten up some plain avocado dishes with an attractive leaf design. Such dishes are ideal for decorating as, although functional, they tend not to be used daily. Also, because you eat from the skin of the avocado, you are unlikely to scratch the design with your cutlery. Decorate the dishes with multi-purpose felt tip paint pens. First, draw the outline of the leaves in the bottom of the dish and around the sides.

Fill in half the leaves with the same colour to make a strong image. Then create a broken line of colour around the rim of the dish as shown. For variety, paint each dish in the set a different colour. When the paint is dry, apply a protective coat of ceramic varnish.

Whose been eating my porridge . . . and left footprints all over my plate? You can have great fun decorating china like this, using bird prints, paw prints, wellington boots or even human footprints. To make the paw print plate, first draw a spiral on to the plate as shown with a chinagraph pencil.

Using the spiral as a guide, paint the outline of the prints in black ceramic paint: you will need a very fine paint brush for this. Once the paint has dried, rub off all trace of the chinagraph line.

Colour the centre of the paws with a brightly coloured ceramic paint. When the plate is completely dry, finish off with a protective coat of ceramic varnish.

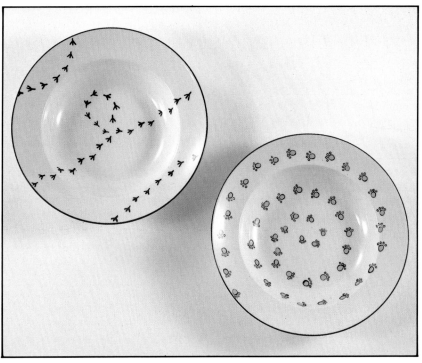

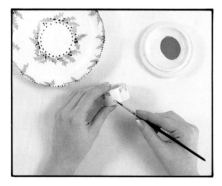

Choose a simple motif, such as holly, mistletoe, or bells, and create your own unique festive tea service. For this attractive holly design, you will need plain white china, red and green ceramic paint and a fine paint brush. Paint the outlines of the holly leaves with green paint, grouping the leaves together in threes. Now fill in the leaf outlines with more green paint.

Join up the leaves with garlands of red berries made by applying dots of red ceramic paint with a very fine brush. Also add clusters of berries at the base of the leaves. When the paint is completely dry, finish off with a coat of ceramic varnish. To complete the picture, you can even paint the motif on to the corner of your paper napkins.

Here's a novel idea for a child's birthday present — a decorative plate complete with birthday cake! Following the design on page 115, draw the image to the required size on some paper, adding the appropriate number of candles to match the age of the child. Then, using a chinagraph pencil, copy the design on to the plate. Leave room for the name at the top of the plate.

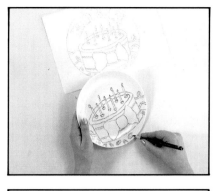

Fill in your design using brightly coloured ceramic paints, mixing the colours to get the required shades. Add white highlights to the blue ribbon to create texture, and surround the flames with little yellow lines to make them glow. For the name, you can either trace some large letters or use transfer lettering.

Put the plate face down on a piece of paper and draw round it in pencil. Then place the letters individually in a semi circle within this outline and stick them down. Trace the name on to some low tack masking peel and stick this on to the plate. Carefully cut out the letters with a craft knife and peel them off. Paint the letters and, when dry, remove the peel. Finally, apply a coat of ceramic varnish.

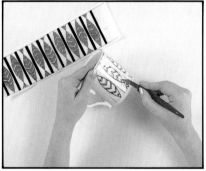

These mugs have been stencilled using low tack masking peel. Choose mugs with straight sides, and not ones which curve out at the top, so that the masking peel will stick properly. Cut out a piece of paper to fit exactly round the mug and, following the templates on page 115, draw the design. Work out your colour scheme using felt tip pens that match the colours of the paints.

Place the low tack peel on top of the design and trace the design on to the peel using an indelible pen. Pull off the backing paper and stick the masking film on to the mug. Then cut out the design with a stencil or craft knife.

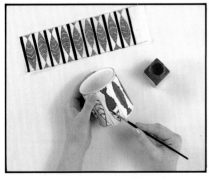

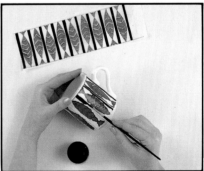

Using ceramic paint and a fine brush, apply the first colour. Try to hold the brush as upright as possible so that you don't get too much seepage under the stencil.

When the paint is dry apply the next colour and so on until the design is complete. Leave to dry, then peel off the masking film. Clean up any rough edges with a stencil knife or a fine brush soaked in turpentine. Finally, apply a coat of ceramic varnish to protect the design.

These octagonal glasses look very stylish with a band of colour rotating around the glass. You will need either ceramic or glass paint. Cut four or five strips of masking tape long enough to wind from the top of the glass down to the bottom. Stick the first strip down then add successive strips, leaving a gap between each one.

Apply the paint to the exposed areas, holding on to the masking tape while you rotate the glass. Now leave the glass to dry.

Remove the masking tape. If some of the paint has seeped under the tape, clean it off with a cloth dipped in turpentine.

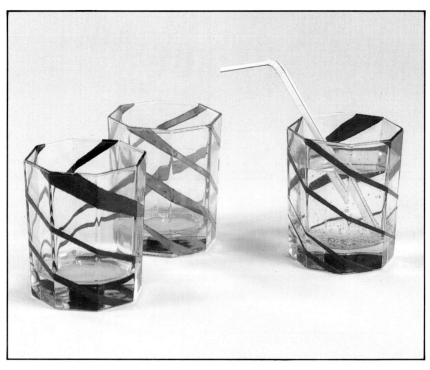

Paris goblets are the cheapest wine glasses you can buy, yet you can transform them into these stylish drinking vessels with no more than a little ingenuity and some glass paints. Working from either the top or the bottom of the glass, paint on a winding plant stem using a fine brush. You may have to leave the glass to dry between painting the bulb and the base so you do not smudge the paint.

Once the stem has dried you can then decorate it with intricate leaves and curling tendrils. Use a very fine brush to achieve a delicate finish.

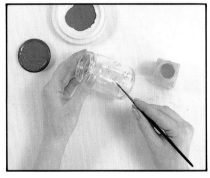

When you buy herbs in jars you are paying more for the packaging than the contents, so why not make your own storage jars and save money? Collect some old glass jars with lids and wash them in hot soapy water, removing any tough labels with a scourer. Dry the jars thoroughly, then use a medium sized artist's brush to paint the lids with ceramic paint.

Using either ceramic or glass paints and a much finer brush, paint a series of tiny yellow dashes in clusters of five to form petals. Leave these to dry.

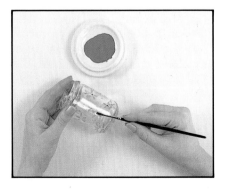

Now dot the flower centres with the same colour of paint you used for the lids. Add the green trellis between the flowers using ceramic or glass paint as before. You may need to apply two coats if using glass paint to achieve a strong colour.

HARVEST STORAGE JARS

Bring the countryside into your kitchen with these charming storage jars. Cut out a piece of paper to fit round the side of the jar and then, using the template on page 116, draw your design on to the paper. To work out your colour scheme, colour the design using felt tip pens. Trace off the design on to the jar and outline the pencil with a fine black felt tip pen.

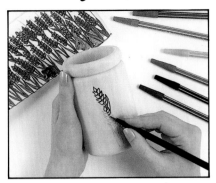

Colour the corn with the coloured felt tip pens, leaving the middle of some of the husks the natural wood colour so that the corn looks more rounded and realistic. Paint the centre of some of the other husks yellow to add more interest. Do not press the pens too hard as the colour will bleed.

Colour in the animals and butterflies and decorate around the top edge of the jar with green, as shown in the main picture, to suggest hills. Paint the lid with swallows soaring in the sunshine and, when the inks are dry, finish with a coat of polyurethane varnish to protect the colour.

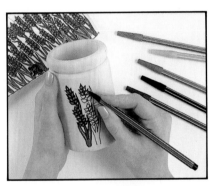

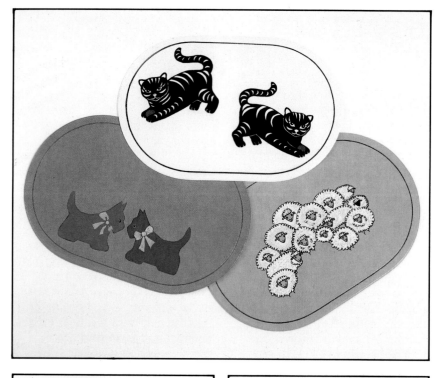

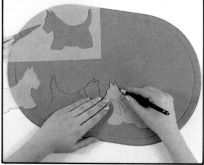 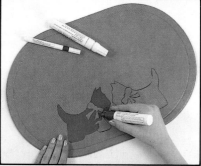

Here's a design the children will love: personalized plate mats delightfully decorated with dogs, cats or even some cute woolly sheep. You can also look at cards, magazines and children's books for images to copy. Either trace your design or draw it free-hand on to some paper. Cut out and draw round your motif on to a plain mat with a chinagraph pencil.

Colour in your image using multi-purpose felt tip pens. If, after you have finished, you have left smudges on your mat, rub them out with lighter fuel. Finish off with a coloured border round the edge of the mat.

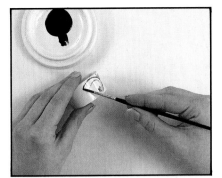

Decorate some napkin rings, and even some napkins, to match your tea or dinner service. You will need ceramic paints that match the colours of your china: in this case blue, green and pink. First, paint the outline of the design using a very fine brush and being careful to make a single sweeping movement with each stroke.

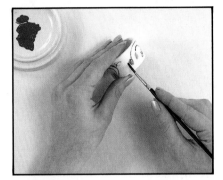

When the initial coat is dry, begin to fill in the outline with a second colour, carefully following the design on your plate.

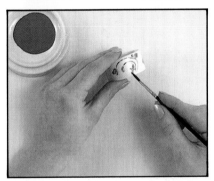

Finish off with a third and, if necessary, a fourth colour, allowing each coat to dry before applying a new one. Protect the design with a coat of ceramic varnish. If you wish to decorate your table napkins as well, follow the same procedure using fabric paints instead of ceramic ones.

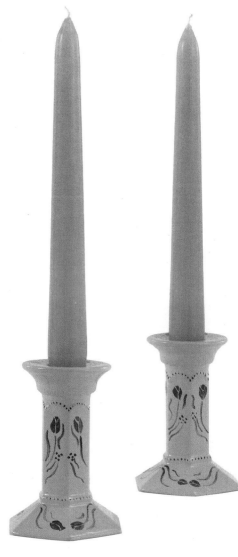

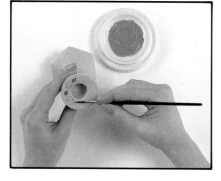

Asimple motif such as a tulip can add style to the plainest of candlesticks. For this design you will need a pair of pink candlesticks, a fine paint brush and some garnet red and green ceramic paints. Decorate the top first, firmly holding the candlestick by the stem as you do so. Begin by painting the red flowers and clusters of tiny red dots, then fill in with green foliage.

Paint the stem and finally the base of the candlestick after the top has dried. Finish with lines of tiny red dots at the top and bottom of the stem, following the shape of the candlestick. Finally, when the paint is completely dry, apply a coat of ceramic varnish.

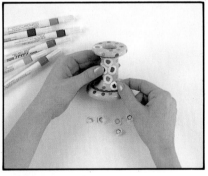

These candlesticks are designed for those in a party mood; they are bright and fun, and especially suitable for a teenage party. You will need some self-adhesive ring reinforcements, candlesticks, and multi-purpose felt tip paint pens in a range of bright colours. Stick the ring reinforcements all over the candlestick as shown.

Paint the centres of the circles in various colours. Once the paint is dry, pull off the reinforcements to reveal a series of coloured dots. Complete the design by painting a border line round the base of the stem in one of the bright colours you have been using. Finally, apply a coat of ceramic varnish.

Crackle varnish creates an interesting 'antique' finish on a prettily decorated wooden salt box. Such boxes can be purchased from specialist craft suppliers at little cost (look in craft magazines for stockists). First, draw your design in pencil on to the pieces of the box. Go over the pencil marks using a fine paint brush and black acrylic paint.

Now fill in the design using brightly coloured acrylic paints, mixing and diluting them with a little water if necessary. Leave the paints to dry thoroughly before pinning the box pieces together.

Cover the box with a coat of patina varnish and leave it to dry for between 4-12 hours before applying a second coat. Once the second coat is dry to the touch (rather than completely dry), paint on a coat of crackle varnish. This should crackle in 15-20 minutes, leaving the box with a crazed, old appearance.

With a design 'borrowed' from the turn of the century, new life has been breathed into some old kitchen scales. To transform your own scales you will need gold and black ceramic paints and some gold spray paint. Clean the surface of the scales with soapy water, then sand down with fine sandpaper. Now apply a coat of black paint; you may need two coats to cover the old finish.

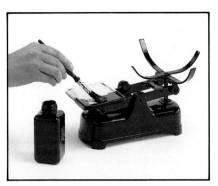

When the black ceramic paint has dried, paint your design in gold using a fine artist's brush. Create the outline first and then fill in with more gold paint. (You may wish to practise your design first on paper before actually applying paint to the scales.)

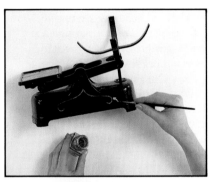

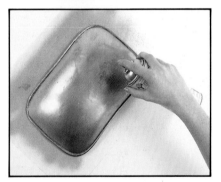

If the scales are purely for a decorative purpose, spray the old dish with gold paint. If they are going to be used for food it is probably better not to paint the dish. Remember always to use spray paints in a well ventilated area.

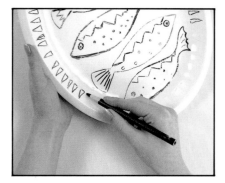

This method of decorating is known as resist painting. To create this primitive design you will need a mixture of glass and ceramic paints. Using a chinagraph pencil, draw the design on to the plate. Remember that whatever areas you cover with the chinagraph will appear white on the finished plate.

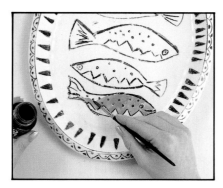

Carefully paint the fish using contrasting ceramic paints. These fish are coloured in deep blue and yellow, but you can try other colour combinations such as purple and orange or black and gold. Now paint the border pattern in bright colours — red looks particularly attractive.

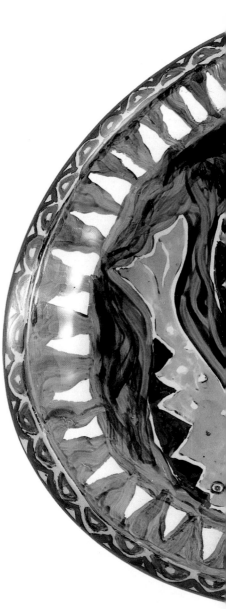

Paint the water surrounding the fish in emerald green glass paint, applying it in an undulating wave pattern to represent water currents. Use glass paint for the water as it is more translucent than ceramic paint. When the paint is completely dry, rub away the chinagraph with a soft dry cloth to reveal the white china.

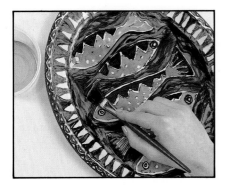

You may need to use a cloth soaked in turpentine to tidy up the edges of the pattern. Finally, protect your design with a coat of ceramic varnish.

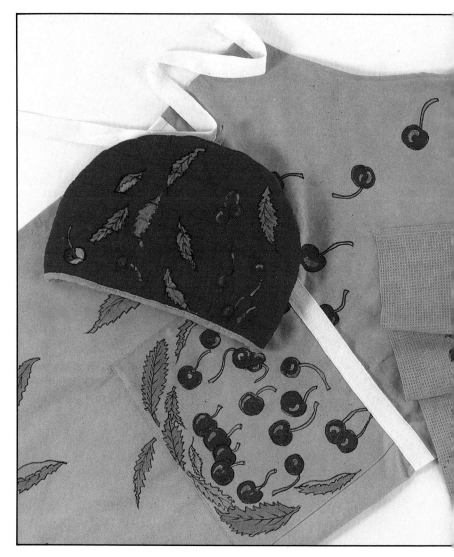

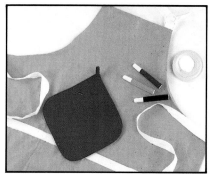 

Co-ordinate your kitchen wear with a simple but effective design of cherries. You will need some fabric felt tip pens and/or some opaque fabric paint plus an apron, tea cosy, pot holder and tea towel to decorate.

Practise the design on some paper first, then, when you are confident, use a fine fabric felt tip pen to draw the outline of your design on to the fabric. Here, the leaves and cherries have been spaced out so that they appear to be tumbling down from the tree. On the apron pocket the leaves are grouped to act as a nest for the falling cherries.

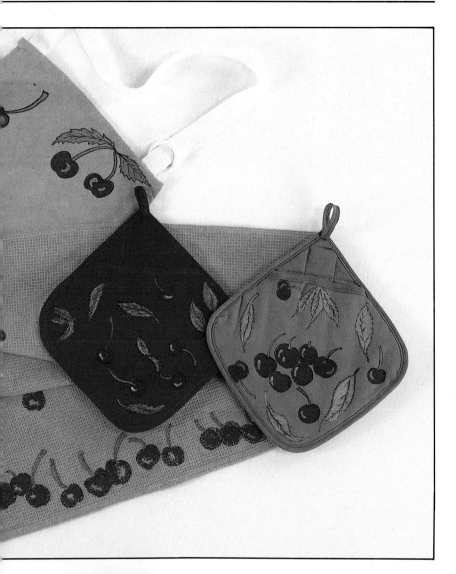

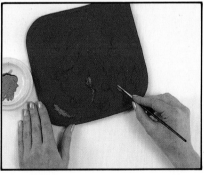

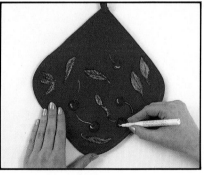

Now fill in the outlines with red and green paint. On dark backgrounds you will need to use opaque paints; these are harder to apply than the felt tip pens, so be patient and keep going over the design to achieve the intensity of colour desired.

When the paint is dry, use the black felt tip pen to add veins to the leaves and shading to the cherries. To complete the design, add white highlights to the cherries. This can be done either with a pen or with the opaque fabric paint. Finally, iron the back of the fabric to fix the paints.

——GIFTS AND NOVELTIES——

In this age of mass-produced goods, there is nothing nicer or more deeply appreciated than receiving a hand-crafted gift, and what could be more original for the person who has everything than the delightful ducks featured below? Equally novel are the decorated Easter eggs on pages 62 and 63, and the colourful clock on page 50 — an ideal gift for a child. Other novelties for the kids include a chopping board transformed into a blackboard and a jazzy school case, designs which the children may enjoy doing themselves. And, finally, to go with your hand-painted gift, why not make your own gift boxes and wrapping papers? You will find a colourful range at the end of the chapter.

Made in the Phillipines from balsa wood, these lovely ornamental ducks are exported all over the world and are widely available in department stores. They are ideal for painting and, as you can see, the end results can be quite stunning. Draw your design on to the duck in pencil, either following one of the designs shown here or using a bird book as reference. Now start to paint.

Acrylic paints are ideal on this surface but you can also use glass or ceramic paints, or even a mixture of all three. Paint the main areas of colour first and then change to a finer brush and fill in details such as the eyes, the white ring round the neck and the markings on the wings and tail.

Finish off with a coat of polyurethane gloss varnish. If you have used a variety of paints remember that they will dry at different rates so make sure they are all dry before varnishing.

A brightly decorated clock makes a novel gift for a child. Self-assembly clocks like this one are available from some craft suppliers (particularly by mail order) so check in craft magazines for stockists. First, sand down the clock so that it is perfectly smooth, then draw your design in pencil. Use bright acrylic paints to colour the design.

When the painting is complete, assemble the clock according to the manufacturer's instructions. Apply a coat of polyurethane varnish for a glossy finish.

Why not have some fun restoring a battered old box and, rather than simply giving it a coat of paint, transform it with a striking black and white leopard skin design? As you can see, this cabinet was originally in a very sorry state with its chipped paint and peeling labels.

First sand the box down, then give it a coat of black ceramic paint. This paint is suitable for metals and gives a shiny finish. If your box is wooden, you can use acrylic paints instead.

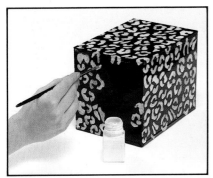

When the black paint has dried, paint the leopard skin markings in white ceramic paint. Look at pictures of leopards and other animals with interesting markings for inspiration. If your box is for stationery, you can even paint some black pens to match.

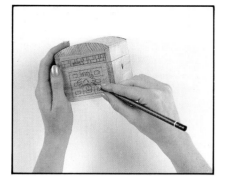

Create this lovely jewellery box, with its lacquer-like finish, from a simple wooden chest. This box was purchased from a craft suppliers (see craft magazines for stockists) but an old wooden box would look just as effective. You will need sand paper, some acrylic paints including black, and some patina varnish. First sand the box until it is perfectly smooth, then draw your design in pencil.

Mix the black acrylic paint with some water to give it a smooth consistency which flows easily. Paint each face of the box in turn, being careful to paint round your design. Paint the sides first and allow to dry before painting the top and bottom — in this way you always have dry surfaces by which to hold the box.

Using a fine brush, paint the details of your design then leave the box to dry. Remember that acrylic paint dries very quickly so wash your brushes in water immediately you have finished with them.

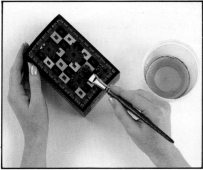

Finally, apply a thin, even coat of patina varnish. As before, do the sides first and leave the box to dry (for 24 hours) before varnishing the rest. Leave the box in a dust free environment while drying. Lightly sand the box with very fine sandpaper before applying another coat: the surface will look dull after sanding, but the gloss will reappear with the second coat.

Transform a pear-shaped chopping board into a novelty blackboard for the children. All you need is blackboard paint and some acrylic paint for the leaves. First draw the leaf design in pencil on to the board.

Now paint the board with the blackboard paint, using a fine brush to paint round the leaf design. The board may need more than one coat of blackboard paint, so allow the first coat to dry before applying the second.

When the paint is dry, apply the colour to the leaves with a fine brush. Finally, give the leaves a coat of varnish to make them shine. Do not varnish the black paint!

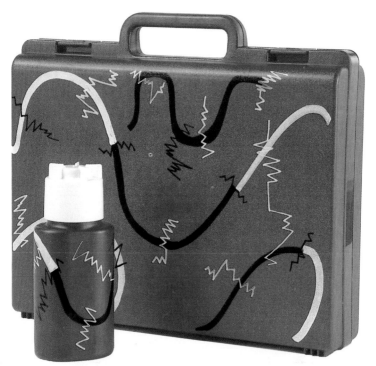

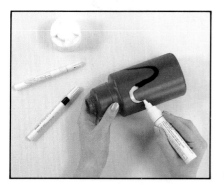 

Here's another idea for the kids — a customized school bag and flask. All you need are the case and flask and some multi-purpose felt tip paint pens. Choose striking colour combinations such as the red, white and black used here. In a strong sweeping movement, paint a deep wavy line using a thick pen. Change pens and finish the curve in a contrasting colour.

Add more wavy lines, alternating colours as before. Then, using a fine pen, draw zig-zag lines cutting across the curved lines. Finally, change pens and draw more zig-zag lines in the second colour.

IT'S A FRAME UP!

The frame you put a picture in can be as important as the picture itself. Frames can be expensive so it's worthwhile spending a little time renovating old ones. The small frame here was new but very plain. The black one needed repainting, with new gilt edging, and the third frame needed filling.

The design inspiration for the small frame was papier mâché frames and boxes made in India. Give the frame a coat of black ceramic paint and then leave it to dry. Now paint the floral design using a gold multi-purpose felt tip paint pen.

Apply a coat of black paint to the mount also. Paint the floral design in gold as before, completely covering the mount, and finish off by filling in the design with deep blue acrylic paint.

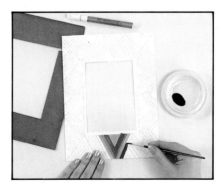

The large frame with the gold edge was simply repainted in black ceramic paint and the edge was outlined in gold. A new cardboard mount was cut and painted with silk paints and a gold felt tip pen, providing a very colourful surround to the picture. The final frame was filled at the joints with wood filler and sanded down, then painted to match the flowers in the picture it holds.

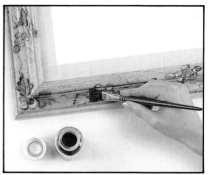

A vine leaf design is used to enhance a plain mirror frame. The design can be painted with acrylic or a combination of ceramic and glass paints, using different shades of green, plus brown, white, yellow and black. Protect the glass before you start painting with a layer of paper stuck down around the edges with masking tape.

To age the frame, stain it with brown and green glass paint diluted with turpentine. When the stain is dry, finish with a coat of varnish. Another way of ageing the frame is to use the 'crackle' varnish method as described on page 42.

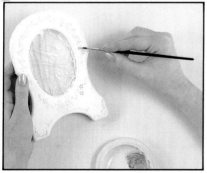

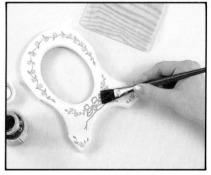

This pretty little frame is perfect for standing on a dressing table. Firstly, sand the frame until it is smooth and then give it a coat of white acrylic paint. Apply a second coat of paint if necessary and, when dry, draw the design with a soft pencil. Paint the design using acrylic paint in soft blues and greys with the flower centres in bright yellow.

Remove the backing and the glass and give the frame a protective coat of polyurethane varnish.

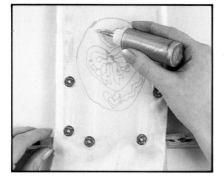 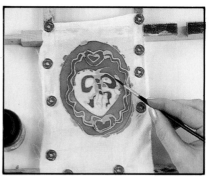

If you really love someone, you'll want to send him a beautiful Valentine's Day card, hand-crafted by you. To make it easier, you can buy the card blanks in most craft shops or haberdashery departments. The designs here are painted on silk. Stretch a piece of white silk over a frame (available from craft shops) and outline the design with gold gutta (see page 18).

Make sure the gutta lines are continuous so that the paint can't bleed through once the design is painted on. When the gutta is dry, apply the silk colours with a fine brush. Do not be over generous with the paint as the silk can only take so much before it is saturated and the colours start to bleed.

When the silk is dry, fix it according to the paint manufacturer's instructions. Then glue the silk in position on to the blank card and stick the mount down around it.

Here's an attractive way to add sparkle to the Christmas tree. You can buy these plain glass balls from craft suppliers, so look in craft magazines for stockists or try your nearest craft shop. As you are decorating a curved surface, it is advisable to keep the design simple. Draw the outlines of your design using a fine multi-purpose felt tip paint pen.

Try to place the motifs evenly, remembering you will see the far side of the design through the glass ball. Fill in the design with the same colour you used for the outlines. You can rub out any mistakes with a cloth soaked in turpentine.

Outline your motifs in a contrasting colour, combining colours such as red and green, yellow and black, pink and purple. Add tiny dots between the motifs using the same colour as that used for the outline. Hang the baubles from your tree with gold gift wrapping thread.

Here's a delightful and unusual way to decorate eggs for Easter Day. As well as eggs, you will need fabric dye, some old fine denier stockings or tights, thread and a varied range of small leaves, the smaller the better. Fill a saucer with water and dip the leaves into the water. Stick the wet leaves on to the eggs (the water will make them adhere).

Cut a piece of stocking large enough to more than cover the egg. Wrap it tightly around the egg to hold the leaves in place, and tie the ends securely in a bundle with a piece of thread.

Mix up the dye according to the maker's instructions and place it in an old saucepan to boil. Gently lower the eggs into the saucepan of simmering dye and cook for about 20 minutes. Drain the eggs and put them under a cold tap. Then remove the stocking and leaves; you will find the leaf shapes imprinted on the shells.

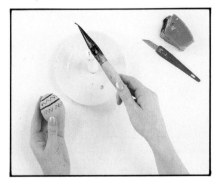

Egg decorating for Easter is particularly popular in Slavonic countries. For this method you must boil the eggs before decorating them. You will need beeswax, some fabric dye, a candle and a tjanting (a Javanese tool designed for painting fine wax lines). Mix the dye according to the maker's instructions. Put a piece of wax in the tjanting and hold it over the candle to melt.

Draw the design on to the egg with your tjanting. Leave the wax to cool before putting the eggs into the dye. (The dye must be completely cold before the eggs are immersed in it.) Check the eggs every few minutes until you are pleased with the colour. Take the egg out of the dye and gently rub off the wax with a cloth. If the wax proves difficult to remove, hold the egg in hot water to melt it.

Gift wrapping can prove so expensive these days, so why not make your own gift boxes? Here, some plain cardboard boxes have been covered in hand-marbled paper. Fill a large bowl with water, then mix some solvent-based paint such as ceramic paint, or some artist's oil colours, with a little white spirit. Use a paint brush to drop successive colours on to the surface of the water.

Stir the mixture with the handle of your paint brush or an old stick until you have a pleasant swirling pattern. An alternative way to form a pattern is to blow the paint across the surface of the water.

Wearing rubber gloves to protect your hands, put the paper on to the surface of the water, then lift it off immediately. The swirls of paint on the paper will create a marbled effect. When the paper is dry, neatly cover a small box, carefully folding the paper round the corners and sticking it down with glue or double-sided tape.

STENCILLED GIFT BOXES

Decorate some pretty boxes with stencils and stencil crayons. You can either buy the stencils from a craft shop or make your own. Position the stencil over the box lid and tape it firmly in place. Now rub a little stencil crayon on to one corner of the film. Pick up some colour with a stencil brush and apply it to the stencil cutout with a circular motion, starting at the edge and working inwards.

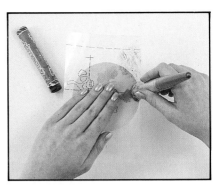

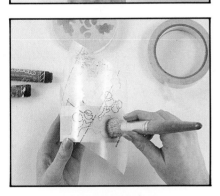

Once you have finished the first colour, change stencils and apply the second colour. Use a clean brush at this stage or your colours will appear muddy.

After you have completed the lid, stencil the sides of the box. Be sure to tape the film firmly in position to stop it from slipping.

GIFT WRAPPING PAPER

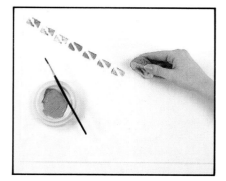

Save the expense of buying wrapping paper by decorating your own. There are many ways to decorate papers: this design is a simple potato print. Cut the potato in half and then sculpt it with a sharp knife so that your motif stands proud. Apply paint to the motif with a brush and then print the colour on to the paper, creating a regular pattern. Re-apply the paint as necessary.

This design is done by ragging. Pour the paint into a container and dip a soft cloth into it. Dab off any excess paint on to waste paper, then apply the first colour in a random manner. Repeat the procedure with a second and even a third colour.

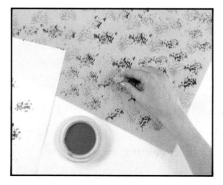

This paper is decorated by sponging, first with gold paint, then with a mid blue and finally with pink. Pour some paint into a container and dip a small natural sponge lightly into the paint. Remove any excess paint by dabbing the sponge on to waste paper, then apply the paint to your paper with light dabbing movements.

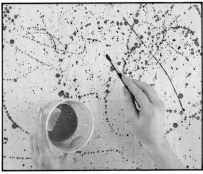

This flicked or splattered design is achieved by flicking paint over the paper. Use a fine brush and flick on the first colour, in this case metallic grey. If you want a variety of marks change the thickness of the brush. Create other designs by drawing wavy lines with felt tip pens, or tracing round a novelty pastry cutter (such as the teddy bear shape above).

FABRIC PAINTING

The popularity of fabric painting has grown rapidly in recent years. This is partly due to the many new materials on the market and the ease with which they can be applied; it also reflects people's desire to express their individuality. You will find in this chapter many different types of painted fabrics, from deckchair covers, blinds and curtains to boxer shorts, silk scarves and leather neck ties. You can decorate fabrics with simple potato-cut prints or fabric felt tip pens, or even try your hand at the stunning art of silk painting (see page 18 for details). Some of the projects featured are very inexpensive, others are more costly, but all will prove worth the time, expense and effort entailed.

Here's a colourful way to transform an old deck chair. Remove the old canvas and fill any holes in the frame with wood filler. Sand down any rough wood until smooth. Apply a coat of primer, followed by one of undercoat, then finish with a brightly coloured gloss paint. Be sure to let each coat dry thoroughly before applying the next one.

You will need some new deck chair canvas to replace the old fabric, plus a white fabric pencil and some opaque fabric paints in a wide range of colours. First draw your design on to the canvas with the fabric pencil, referring to the template on page 117.

Paint the canvas using the opaque paints, cleaning your brush carefully between each colour. Paint the fish in bright colours and lively patterns; outline and segment the shells in gold and the star fish in bright reddy-orange. Iron the fabric on the back to fix the colours then tack the canvas on to the deck chair frame.

You probably think of potato printing as something you used to do in primary school — well think again! It can be used to great effect when decorating soft furnishings for the home. Cut a potato in half and draw the design on to one half with a felt tip pen. Now cut around the motif so that the design stands proud of the background.

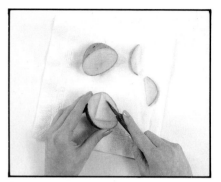

Paint some fabric paint on to the potato motif with a brush. Stamp off an excess paint on to some waste paper then print the motif on to your chosen fabric, leaving plenty of space for a second and even a third motif.

Cut another simple motif from the other half of the potato. Apply the colour as before and print on to the fabric. When the fabric has dried, iron on the back to fix the paints. Your fabric is now ready to be made up into cushions, curtains, blinds and so forth.

These cushions are based on designs taken from American patchwork quilts. With a soft pencil, copy the design on to tracing paper then position the trace, pencil marks down, over your chosen fabric. Transfer the image on to the fabric by tracing over the back of the design.

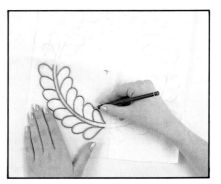

When the design is on the material, go over it with a pencil if the image is not strong enough. Apply the first colour using a fabric felt tip pen.

Fill in the other colours. If you are using alternate colours, as on these leaves, it is a good idea to mark each leaf with the correct colour so you don't make a mistake half way through. Iron on the back to fix the design and make the fabric up into cushions.

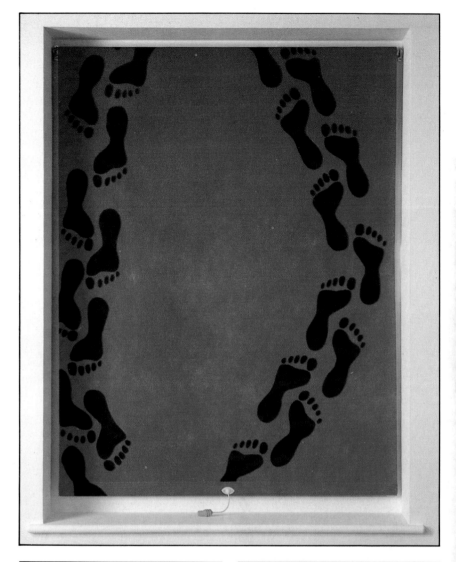

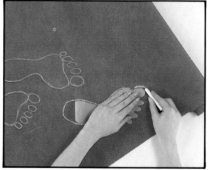
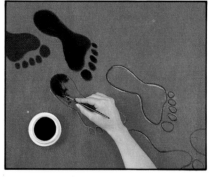

This is a very simple but effective design for a blind. All you need is a plain blind, some chalk, black fabric paint, a black fabric felt tip pen and your own two feet! Draw round your foot on tracing paper and cut out the shape. Use this as a template to draw feet on to the blind with chalk, drawing the toes individually as shown. Keep turning the template over to get left and right footprints.

When you have chalked your design going up and down the blind, draw over the chalk with a black fabric pen. Fill in the centre of each foot with black fabric paint then iron on the reverse side of the fabric to fix the colour.

Forget city life and make-believe you live in a cottage by the sea with this colourful blind. A photograph of a sea gull is a useful reference when drawing the bird. Create your design at a reasonable size first then square it up to full size (see page 14) so that it fits on the blind. Draw the design on to a plain white blind in pencil.

When painting such a complex picture, it is a good idea to paint the background first, so start with the sky. This is a mixture of white and blue fabric paint, sponged on quite densely. The clouds are sponged on more lightly. Once the background is painted, start painting in the details. When you've finished, iron the back of the fabric to fix the paints.

These attractive full-length curtains will add style to any modern living room and can be painted in any colour to match the decor. You will need lots of space when painting the fabric so cover your floor with plenty of newspaper before you begin. Now rip sheets and sheets of newspaper into long strips. It is best to use quality newspapers as they are wider and have more pages.

Sew together enough fabric to make a curtain and lay it out on the floor. Tape several strips of newspaper together so that they fit across the width of your fabric. Now, using loops of masking tape on the underside of the paper, stick the strips to the cloth, leaving gaps between the rows. As you work your way towards the top of the cloth, break up the rows with small 'islands' of paper.

Pour some opaque black fabric paint on to a saucer or plate and, starting at the bottom of the cloth, sponge the paint between the rows of newspaper.

With each new row, mix a little white opaque fabric paint into the black before you dip the sponge in. Keep adding white with each successive row so that the colour gradually changes from black to grey as you print up the cloth. By the time you get to the top where you have the islands of paper the colour should be light grey.

Leave the fabric paint to dry before removing the paper. Repeat the whole procedure with the second curtain. Iron on the back of each piece of fabric to fix the colour and then make them up into curtains.

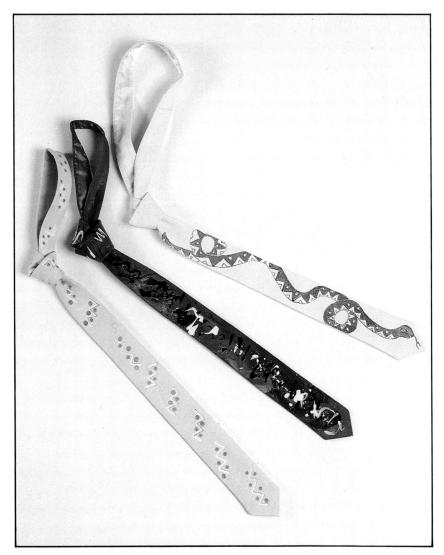

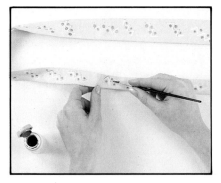

T̲ake a leather tie, some opaque leather dyes and plenty of imagination! Leather dyes are simple to use — just paint them on with a fine brush — and you can create any style you wish, from the modest to the outrageous. The pink tie has a simple zig-zag pattern drawn on in white with deep pink spots circled in blue. Be sure to clean the brush thoroughly between each different colour.

To create this tie, sponge the leather with a mixture of blue and black dye. Then use a paint brush to flick white, blue and black leather dyes all over the surface. The white tie has been decorated with a coiled serpent.

Create a unique gift for the man in your life by decorating a pair of boxer shorts with fabric felt tip pens. Draw your design on to paper first, referring to the template on page 116 if your wish to create this busy design. Work out your colour scheme by colouring in your design with felt tip pens.

Place a piece of card between the front and the back of the shorts to stretch the waist band and stop the paint seeping through. Draw the design on to the fabric using a fine fabric felt tip pen. If you don't feel confident drawing the design straight on in pen, trace it on in pencil first.

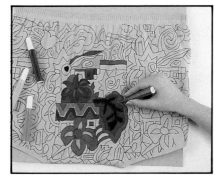

Colour in the design in bright colours, using either fabric felt tip pens or fabric paint and a brush. To fix the paint, iron on the back of the fabric once your design is complete.

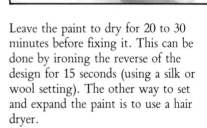

These Grecian-style tee shirts are decorated with a paint that expands upon heating, so that the design is raised above the surface of the fabric. First, draw your design on to a piece of paper. Then stick the design on to a piece of cardboard and stretch the tee shirt over the card, fastening the fabric down with masking tape. Trace the design on to the tee shirt using the 'expanding medium' paint.

Leave the paint to dry for 20 to 30 minutes before fixing it. This can be done by ironing the reverse of the design for 15 seconds (using a silk or wool setting). The other way to set and expand the paint is to use a hair dryer.

This colourful design is applied using transfer paints. As well as the paints, you will also need a piece of non-absorbent paper, such as tracing paper, and an iron. Draw your design on to the paper, referring to the template on page 118, and making sure it will fit on to the scarf you wish to decorate.

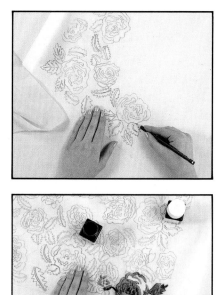

Colour in your design with the transfer paints in the same way as you would using any water-based paints. Mix the colours together and dilute them with water as you wish.

Leave the paints to dry for an hour then place the design face down on the scarf so that the paint is against the fabric. Set your iron to the cotton setting and iron on the back of the paper for one minute so that the colour is transferred. When the paper has cooled, remove it from the scarf.

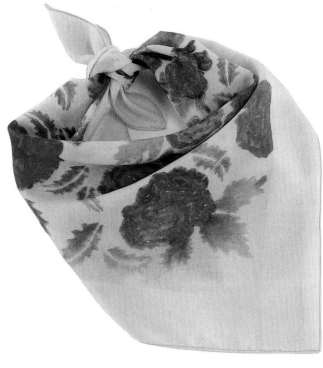

Silk painting is very much easier than it looks and, once hooked, you will find it not only a satisfying hobby but also a wonderful source of presents for friends and family. Either draw the design on page 119 to the required size or trace over a design you wish to copy, such as a picture in a magazine or book.

Using silk pins, stretch your length of silk over a frame. (Easily assembled frames for silk painting are readily available from craft shops.) Tape the design to the frame underneath the silk so that you can see it clearly through the fabric.

Fill an applicator with gutta (see page 18) and trace over the lines of the design, making sure that all the lines are completely joined; any gaps will allow the silk paint to bleed through. Leave the gutta to dry for about an hour before applying the silk colours.

Use a soft brush to apply the paint. Place your colour-loaded brush between the lines of gutta and let the colour creep up to the lines. Rinse the brush in water before using the next colour so that you don't end up with muddy hues. Once you have completed your design and the paints are dry, iron on the back of the silk to fix the colours. Your scarf is now ready to hem.

INTERIOR DESIGN

In recent years it has become highly fashionable to use a decorative paint technique on walls. To have such finishes painted professionally can be a very expensive affair, so why not be adventurous and paint your own? In this chapter you will find three of the simplest and most effective techniques — stippling, sponging and ragging — all of which can be done using ordinary emulsion paints. To make things easier still, you can even buy kits that contain all the necessary items to help you achieve a perfect finish. Other designs featured include two highly original wall light decorations, a delightful stencilled border based on an Egyptian frieze, and some colourful lamps and vases.

Stippling is a paint technique which gives an attractive soft finish, made up with a myriad of tiny dots of colour. The wall below is stippled with emulsion paint in two shades of blue — forget-me-not and moon shadow — on a lavender white base. Begin by applying the base colour with a roller or brush, giving two coats if necessary.

Stippling brushes are wide with a large number of bristles and, traditionally made from badger hair, they are quite expensive to buy. As an alternative you could try using a brush or broom. Lightly dip the brush into your paint so that only the very ends of the bristles are covered. Then apply the paint to the walls with a very light touch so as not to blur the image.

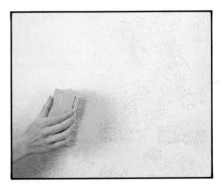

Evenly cover the wall with the first colour, trying not to overlap the stippling. Wash your brush and leave it to dry before applying the second colour as before. Fill in any spaces and overlap the previously stippled areas. Before you take on a whole room, experiment on one small area first to perfect your technique.

Sponging is one of the easiest paint finishes to achieve. You can use one, two or more colours. When choosing colours, go for a light, mid and darker shade of the same colour. Here, rose white has been used as a base for soft peach and dusky apricot. It is a good idea to buy some small samples of emulsion paint to practise with before you start. First, apply the base coat with a brush or roller.

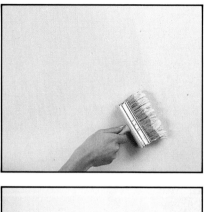

When your base colour is dry, take a natural sponge and dampen it. Now dip the sponge into the second colour, being careful not to overload it with paint. Remove any excess paint by dabbing the sponge on to waste paper, then apply paint to the walls with a light dabbing motion. Don't press hard or the paint will smudge. Continue in a random pattern, re-applying paint to the sponge as necessary.

Wash out your sponge and apply the third colour, overlapping the second colour. When you have finished you should have an even blending of the three colours. If the last colour is too dominant you can soften it by sponging over with some of the base colour.

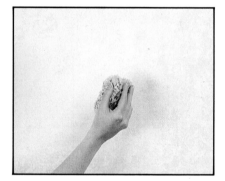

There are two main methods of ragging: 'ragging off', in which you apply rags to a wet wall of paint, so removing the colour and leaving a pattern; or 'ragging on' as shown here. In the latter, the colour is applied with bunched-up rags, in a similar way to sponging. First apply a base coat of emulsion paint with a roller or a brush.

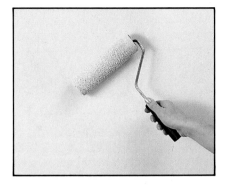

Use dry rags for this technique — it is the crisp folds in the fabric that form the pattern. Make sure you cut up lots of rags before you start and have plenty of waste paper around. Clasp a rag in your hand and dip it lightly into the paint. Dab off the top layer of paint on to some waste paper, then apply the cloth to the wall with a dabbing motion.

Continue to apply paint in a random pattern, replacing the rag with a fresh one as soon as it becomes too damp. When the first colour has dried, apply a second colour as before: a contrasting colour can look particularly effective.

In this colourful design, a wall light is transformed into an umbrella bursting with toys. First mark the segments of the umbrella by putting strips of masking tape on to the shade as shown and ruling down one edge of each strip with a multi-purpose felt tip paint pen. Remove the tape and colour each segment using acrylic paints. Draw an outline of the shade on to the wall.

Draw the various elements of the design in pencil on to tracing paper — restrict your shapes to balloons, balls and kites if you are not too confident about more complex shapes. Pencil over the reverse of each trace and transfer the images on to the wall. As before, use acrylic paints to colour in the toys. Complete the picture by fixing the shade in position.

For those of you who like plants but lack green fingers, why not paint your own plant, cascading down from a wall lamp. Make an outline of your shade on to the wall so you know where to position the plant. Now, using a house plant as reference, draw the design on to the wall. Use a pencil so you can rub out any mistakes.

If you are using a translucent lightshade like this one, you can draw some of the leaves within the outline so that they show through the shade. Paint the leaves using acrylic paints or even artist's oils, though the latter will take a little longer to dry. Use dark colours to create shadow and depth, and light colours to add highlights. Finally, fix your shade in place. As you can see, the effect is stunning.

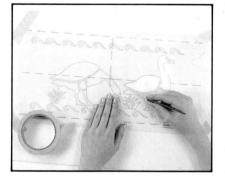

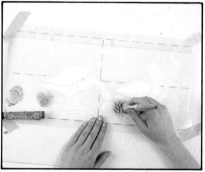

This stencil border is inspired by a 3rd century BC Egyptian painting. First, draw the design on page 120 to the required size, referring to the instructions on squaring up on page 14. With masking tape, attach some stencil film over the design and cut out the shapes using a stencil or craft knife.

You can stencil with either paint or crayons. Stencil crayons have been used here as they give a soft effect, similar to spraying. Position the stencil over your border and tape it in place. Now rub some crayon on to one corner of the stencil film and then dip the brush into the colour. Apply the colour to the area you wish to stencil using a circular motion.

Lighter shades should be applied first, with darker tones added on top to provide shading and depth of colour. It is a good idea to use a separate brush for each colour so that you do not get a muddy effect.

To finish the stencil, colour in the border design in a slightly stronger terracotta colour. Draw the eyes on to the geese using a pencil. When you have finished one section of the border, move the stencil along to the next area and repeat the process. Once you are confident at stencilling, as an alternative to painting a border, you can paint straight on to the wall.

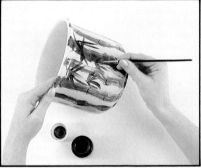

Decorate a plain ceramic planter with bamboo stems and leaves, painted in a Chinese style. You will need green and yellow ceramic paint and green and black glass paint. Paint wide vertical lines of green around your pot, using a 20mm (¾in) decorator's brush and both the glass and the ceramic paints to give different depths of colour. Make the lines uneven and slightly crooked.

Add yellow highlights to some of the green stripes. Mix some green and a little black paint and, with a fine pointed brush, paint slightly curved horizontal lines at intervals across the vertical lines. Finally, using a soft pointed Chinese art brush and the green/black mix, paint groups of leaves radiating out from the stems.

The inspiration for this vase comes from a beautiful piece of Victorian embroidery. The designs are similar except the white and black have been reversed so, instead of white stalks on a black background, there are black stalks on a white background. You can either copy this design, or find a similar piece of embroidery to copy.

As it is always difficult to paint directly on to a curved surface, first draw the design on to the vase using a chinagraph pencil.

Colour in the design with ceramic paints, mixing the various colours together to get the right shades. Use very fine paint brushes for the stalks and slightly thicker ones for the leaves and flowers. Clean the brushes carefully between each colour.

With a combination of ragging and flicking you can transform a plain china vase or jug into a work of art. You will need a piece of cloth for the ragging, a couple of fine artists' brushes and some ceramic paints. Dip the rag into one of the paints and then blot it onto some waste paper to remove any excess paint. Now begin to dab paint on to the vase.

Leave gaps between the dabs of paint to allow the background colour to show through. When you have evenly covered the surface, leave it to dry. Now spatter the vase with white ceramic paint, flicking the paint on with a fine brush. Once again, leave to dry.

Finally, apply some gold ceramic paint with a fine paint brush, forming clusters of little gold dots across the surface of the vase. Be sure to clear your brush thoroughly in turpentine when you have finished.

An elegant but inexpensive vase is transformed with the simple use of a sponge and some ceramic paints. Take a small piece of natural sponge and dip it into some white spirit. Squeeze the sponge out and lightly dip it into a saucer of ceramic paint. Dab excess paint on to a piece of waste paper, then apply the colour to the vase with a light dabbing motion.

Sponge the whole of the vase, leaving space for a second colour, and re-applying paint to the sponge as necessary. Use a second sponge to apply the next colour, making sure to overlap the colours for an even finish. As an alternative to ceramic paints, you could use high gloss gold lacquer and ordinary emulsion paint.

A plain lampshade is decorated with a simple ivy motif, coloured in with pearlized fabric paints. First, draw the design on to tracing paper, then pencil over the shapes on the reverse side. Tape the trace in position over the shade and transfer the design by following the outline once more.

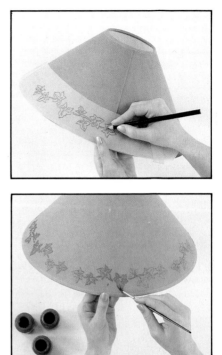

Go over the motif in pencil to make the images stronger. When this is done you can colour in the design. If you cannot buy pearlized fabric paint, use opaque fabric paint on dark background colours, or ordinary fabric paints on light backgrounds. When the design is complete, fix the colour by holding the shade under a hot hair dryer for a few minutes.

The inspiration for this lamp came from a small evening bag. Either copy the design used here or find an alternative source of inspiration, such as a piece of fabric, a greeting card or a porcelain plate. Then experiment with the colours you are going to use, colouring in the design with felt tip pens.

Trace your design on to the shade and colour it in using brightly coloured fabric felt tip pens. Edge the motifs in stronger colour. Now paint the design on to the lamp base using ceramic paints. If you do not feel confident about painting the shapes straight on to the surface, draw them on first with a chinagraph pencil.

Leave the first colour to dry before edging the design in a lighter shade. You will need to fix the paint on the lampshade by heating it with a hair dryer for a few minutes.

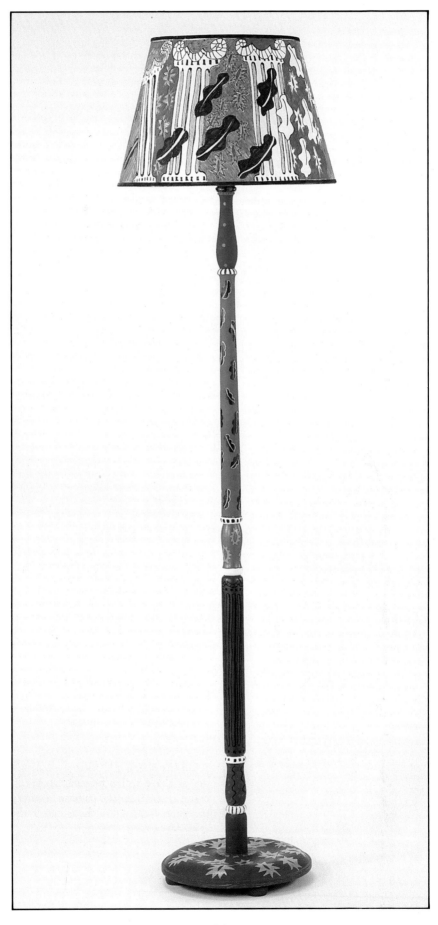

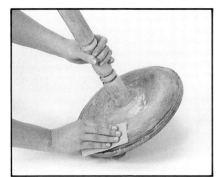

Here's something for those who enjoy the outrageous and the avant garde — an old standard lamp eye-catchingly decorated with Doric columns and oak leaves. Following the maker's instructions, strip the original finish off the lamp-stand with varnish remover. Use an old toothbrush to get into difficult corners. Rub down the surface with wire wool then sand it to give a smooth finish.

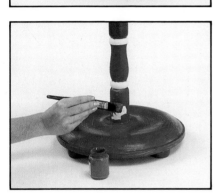

Paint the stand with primer and, when this is dry, apply some undercoat. Alternatively, you could use two coats of combined primer/undercoat. Leave the stand to dry before you begin to apply the colour.

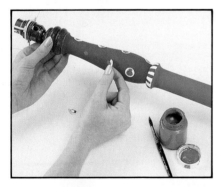

Decorate the standard lamp with acrylic paints, using bold, primary colours. Paint different parts of the lamp different colours, and break the colours up with rings of white, using the carved features as guidelines.

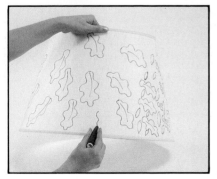

Now decorate the base colours with dots, dashes, spots, leaves and columns, using both acrylic paints and multi-purpose felt tip paint pens. Paint the spots by sticking ring reinforcements on to one section of the stand and filling in the holes with a brightly contrasting colour. Paint black oak leaves on another section and outline them in bright yellow using the felt tip pens.

When the stand is dry, apply a coat of protective varnish. Outline your design on the shade with a fine line fabric felt tip pen, repeating the patterns used on the stand. Now fill in the design with thick fabric pens, continuing to use brightly contrasting colours.

FURNITURE

A book on decorative painting would not be complete without a section on furniture. Some of the items in this chapter are new, but the majority are old, unfashionable pieces that have been given new life with an ingenious paint finish. When renovating an old piece of wooden furniture, make sure it is worth the time and effort you are about to invest — check carefully for woodworm before you begin. Also remove any broken nails and large splinters, especially if the piece is to be used by children. Make sure you are adequately protected when using paint and varnish strippers: these substances are caustic and can cause nasty burns if they come into contact with the skin.

PRETTY PASTEL COT

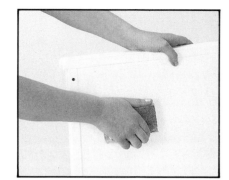

New cots can be expensive, so why not give an old one a face lift with a new coat of paint? But rather than simply painting it all one colour, use a range of pretty pastel shades to create a stylish effect. Before you begin painting, dismantle the cot and replace any loose bars with dowelling of the required diameter. Then sand the old surface down so it is smooth.

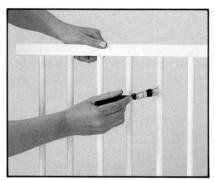

If necessary, give the cot a coat of undercoat. In pencil, number each bar according to the colour you intend to paint it — in this case the numbers one to three represent pink, yellow and blue respectively. Using lead free nursery paint, colour the bars according to the numbers, finishing one colour before cleaning the brush and starting the next. Apply a second coat if necessary once the first has dried.

Using the same three paints, paint the inside of the cot ends in one colour and the outside in another. Now choose a fourth, stronger shade to paint the surrounds on both the ends and sides of the cot. Apply a second coat as necessary.

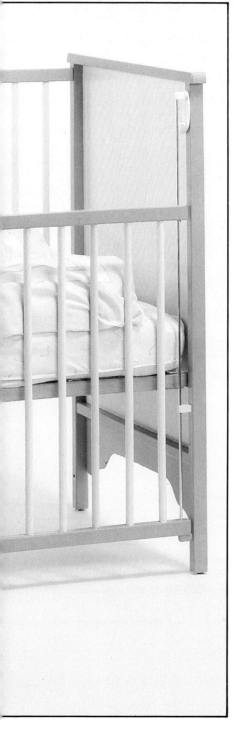

A n old chest of drawers is stripped
down and given new life with a
beautiful rose motif. The idea works
just as effectively on modern pine
furniture. If necessary, strip off the old
finish with varnish remover or paint
stripper, according to the manufacturer's instructions. Use an old toothbrush to get into difficult corners. Rub
the wood down with wire wool and
then sand it until it is smooth.

Draw the design on to tracing paper,
referring to the template on page 121.
Draw variations on this design for the
back plate and centre drawer. Either
trace the design on to the furniture or
cut it out and draw round the shape,
filling in the detail afterwards.

Start to paint the design with acrylic
paints, mixing the colours well so that
you have a wide range of shades and
tones. Use darker shades to create
shadow and depth, and light shades,
including a touch of white, to add
highlights.

When your design is finished and completely dry, apply a coat of varnish to the rose motifs. You can then wax the woodwork, applying several coats of beeswax polish to build up a good finish. Alternatively, you can save your energy by varnishing the entire chest.

Personalize a pine toy chest with your child's name and a delightful array of wild animals. You will find a template of the design on page 122; all you have to do is add the name. Using wire wool and white spirit, remove any wax finish from the box. Wipe the chest down with clean soapy water and, when dry, sand down any rough edges.

Draw the design on to tracing paper, then go over the back of the trace with a pencil. Now tape the design on to the box and trace over the original line. This will only leave a faint mark unless the wood is new, so go over the lines with a pencil or even a fine felt tip pen.

Using acrylic paints, start painting in the design. An old plate or saucer will serve as a palate on which to mix your paints. Try to add tonal variation with light and dark shades, but if you are not happy doing this, keep the colours flat.

When the paint is dry you can strengthen the outlines by drawing round them once more with a pencil or fine felt tip pen. Use a pen or pencil to add fine details such as whiskers, eyes and mouths as well. Finally, give the box a coat of clear varnish. This will not only protect the design but will also make the colours come to life.

An old piece of utility furniture, long past its prime, is transformed with a beautiful paint finish and some new china handles. Choose a light coloured emulsion paint for the base colour, plus a medium and a dark shade for the sponging on. Before you start to redecorate, you will need to remove the old finish.

Place the piece of furniture in a well ventilated room, standing it on plenty of newspaper to protect the surrounding floor. Apply paint stripper according to the manufacturer's instructions; leave for the required length of time and then scrape off the old paint. Wash down the surface with liquid detergent and water and, when dry, sand it until the wood is smooth.

Next, apply a primer, an undercoat and then an emulsion base colour, leaving the cupboard to dry between coats. Take a natural sponge, wet it and squeeze it so it is just damp. Dip it into your second colour and dab any excess paint on to waste paper before applying paint to the cupboard. Use a light dabbing motion so that you do not smudge the paint, and leave lots of gaps for the next colour.

Apply the third and darkest colour with a clean sponge, filling in any gaps and overlapping other sponged areas.

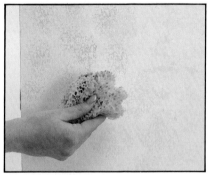

Finally, using ceramic paint, decorate some plain white china handles with a pretty leaf or floral pattern. If you need inspiration for your design, try looking at an old china cup or plate.

A striking 'Mondrian' inspired design in bold colours gives a new lease of life to a battered old director's chair. Even if you don't have an old chair to do up it's still worth buying a new one to customize. As well as paint brushes, masking tape and a sponge, you will also require varnish, acrylic paints, opaque fabric paints and a black fabric paint pen.

Remove the canvas from your chair; if it is old, you can replace it later with new deck chair canvas. Sand down the chair frame until the wood is smooth and fill any cracks with wood filler. Now paint the outline of the frame with black acrylic paint, applying a second coat if necessary.

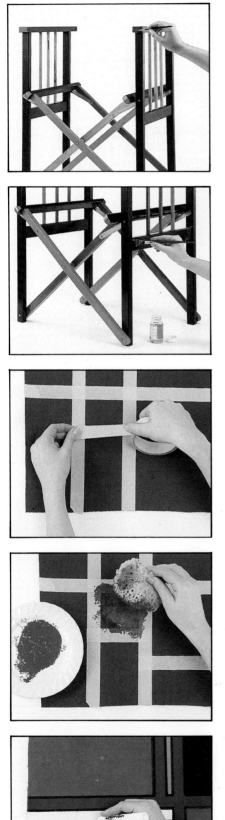

Using red, green and blue acrylic paint and a fine paint brush, paint the cross pieces, the central dowels and the ends of the legs and arms in alternating bright colours. Acrylic paints dry very quickly so clean your brush instantly between each colour.

When the paint is completely dry, give the frame a couple of coats of varnish to protect it. Leave the first coat to dry before applying the second one.

Using either the original covers or some new fabric cut to size, put strips of masking tape across the canvas, masking off a series of rectangles both large and small. Rub the tape down with the back of a spoon to give it extra adhesion.

Pour some opaque fabric paint into a saucer and dip a sponge into the colour. Dab the paint on to a masked area of the canvas being sure not to get any paint on the adjacent squares. Use a sponge rather than a paint brush to avoid brush strokes. When you have finished applying one colour, take a clean sponge and apply the next. Continue like this until all the rectangles are filled in.

You may find you have to use more than one coat of paint if you are working on a very dark background. When the paint is completely dry, tear off all the masking tape. Finish by drawing a black rule round each of the rectangles, using a fabric paint pen. You can now put the canvas back on the chair.

Here's a cheerful way to decorate some inexpensive plastic chairs for a party or kid's playroom. All you need are some fine multi-purpose felt tip pens and a chinagraph pencil. Using the chinagraph pencil, draw your design on to the seat and the back of the chair, creating bold shapes and patterns. Rub out any mistakes with a soft cloth soaked in lighter fuel.

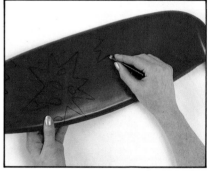

Colour in your outlines with the multi-purpose pens, using brightly contrasting and even clashing colours. Decorate the stars with dots, spots, dashes and triangles of black.

Outline the edges of the shapes in black to make the images sharper. Finally, link up the various elements of your design with colourful streamers and more dots and dashes.

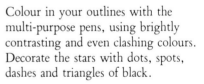

BLOOMSBURY CHAIR

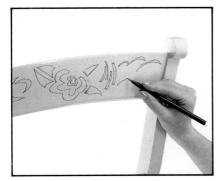

This chair was inspired by designs of the 'Bloomsbury Group' (a London-based group of artists and writers). First, give a plain wooden chair a fresh coat of gloss paint. Then, referring to the pattern in the main photograph, draw the design on to the surface using a fine black felt tip pen.

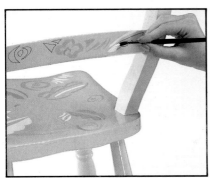

Using gloss paints, colour in the design with a fine brush, making sure you just cover the black outlines so that the design remains soft, rather than hard-edged.

In recent years, Lloyd loom chairs such as this have become collectors' items. But because so many of them are now in poor condition, they are often renovated and painted with an attractive motif. The flamboyance of this design is intended to reflect the warm sunny conservatory for which such chairs were originally intended.

You can either paint the chair using aerosol spray paint or apply paint in the traditional manner with a paint brush. Draw your rose design on to the chair, using a soft pencil and keeping the flowers big and bold. Colour in the design with acrylic paints, mixing the colours to get a wide range of shades. Use dark shades to add shadow and depth, and lighter shades for the highlights.

Bambooing is a simple but effective paint technique which can add interest to a plain piece of cane furniture. Before you start to paint, remove any varnish from your furniture with varnish remover. Dilute some brown acrylic paint with water to make a wash, then, using a 20mm (¾in) brush, paint bands of colour at intervals along the cane.

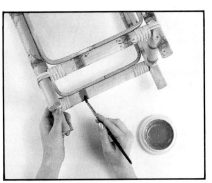

Next, using the same colour undiluted and a fine brush, paint on the markings. First, paint lines of colour in the centre of the band of wash. Next paint elongated 'V' shapes in pairs at right angles to the lines, finishing off with tiny dots by the sides of the Vs. When the bambooing is complete, apply a coat of varnish to protect the paintwork.

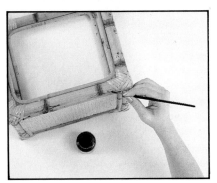

T̲urn a plain wooden pedestal into a stunning marbled plant stand. Stands such as these are available from craft suppliers (look in craft magazines for stockists). Successful marbling requires a lot of practice, so experiment on a spare piece of wood before tackling the real thing. Prime and undercoat the surface as necessary, then apply a coat of black eggshell paint.

Now mix a white tinted glaze using 60% scumble (available from decorating shops) to 20% white eggshell paint and 20% white spirit. Dab the glaze on to the surface with a decorator's brush, allowing plenty of the black to show through.

Rag over the wet glaze with a soft cloth, spreading the glaze to give a dappled effect, and still making sure some of the black shows through. Soften the ragging effect with a stippling brush and a rag dipped in white spirit.

Mix a small quantity of black glaze using the same proportions as before: 60% scumble; 20% black eggshell paint; 20% white spirit. Now use a fine pointed brush to paint on the black veining.

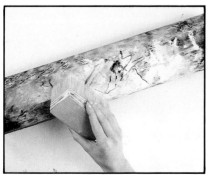

As you finish veining an area, soften the effect with a stippling brush to break up the hard edges. When you have completed the black veining, repeat the process with white glaze, using a stippling brush to soften the edges as before. When the paint is dry, apply a coat of polyurethane varnish to give the glossy cold sheen of marble.

— DESIGN TEMPLATES —

The design templates on the following pages are printed on grids to help you copy them more easily. To reproduce the designs at the required size, refer to the instructions on 'squaring up' which can be found in the introduction on pages 14-15.

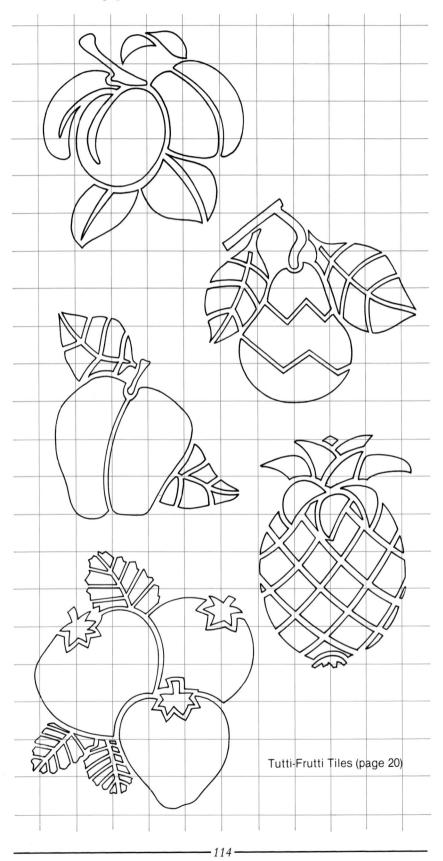

Tutti-Frutti Tiles (page 20)

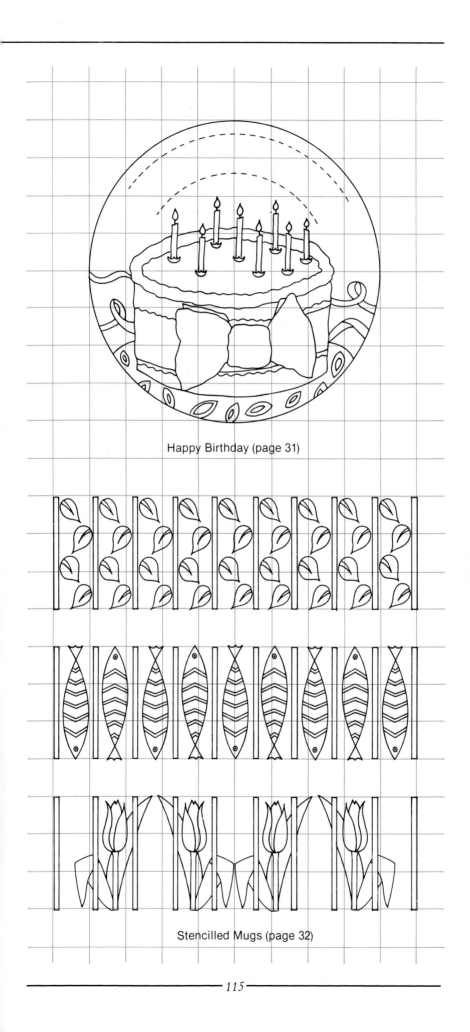

Happy Birthday (page 31)

Stencilled Mugs (page 32)

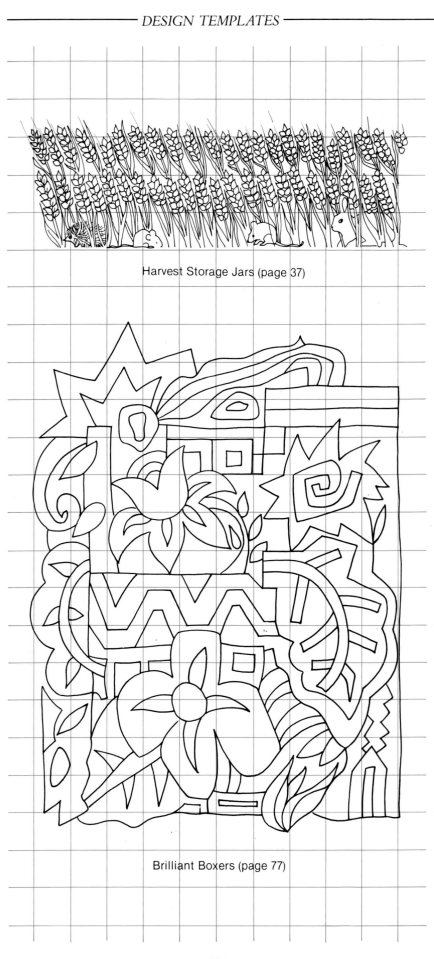

Harvest Storage Jars (page 37)

Brilliant Boxers (page 77)

Rosy Scarf (page 79)

Sea Scape Scarf (page 80)

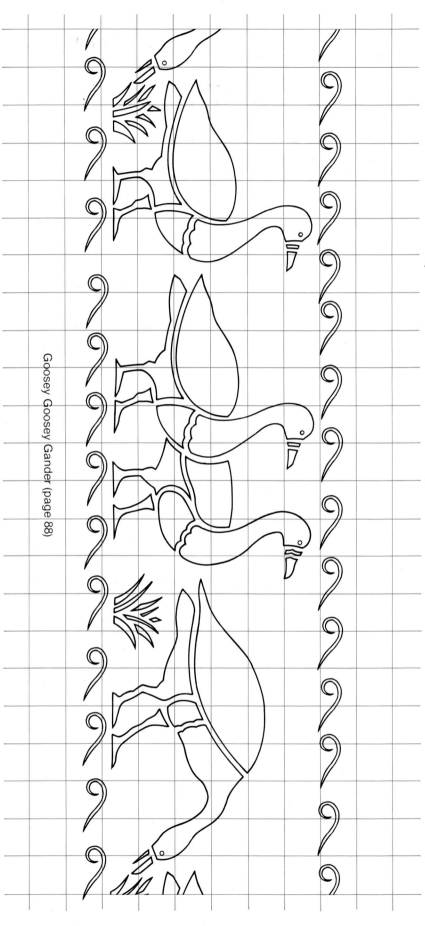

Goosey Goosey Gander (page 88)

Everything's Coming Up Roses (page 100)

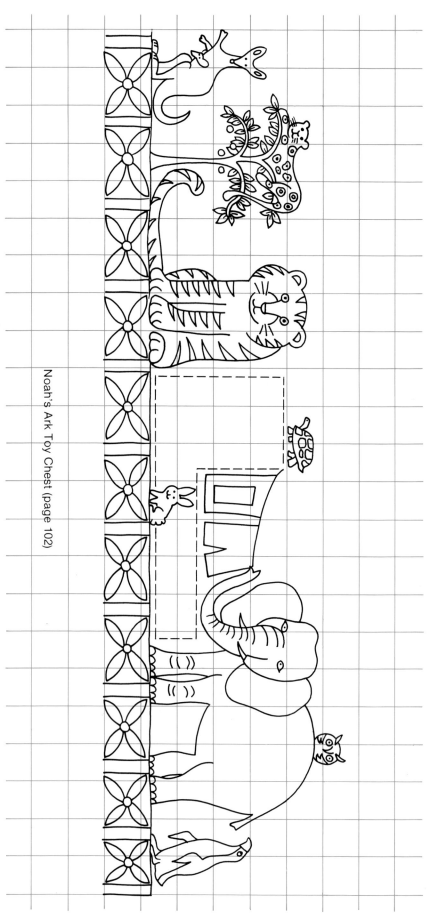

Noah's Ark Toy Chest (page 102)

INDEX

ACKNOWLEDGEMENTS

The author and publishers would like to thank the following for their help in compiling this book:

Bette Rennett and A West and Partners Ltd. for supplying Pebeo paints and brushes.
684 Mitcham Road, Croydon, Surrey.

Shirley Colyer at H W Peel and Co. for supplying paper, paints and brushes.
Norwester House, Fairway Drive, Greenford, Middlesex.

David Constable at Candle Makers Suppliers for supplying the silk and the silk pins.
28 Blythe Road, London W14.

Sunway Blinds for supplying the roller blinds.
Sunway UK Ltd., Mersey Industrial Estate, Heaton Mersey, Stockport, Cheshire.

International Paint for supplying the nursery paint.
Retail Division, 24/30 Canute Road, Southampton, Hampshire.

Panduro Hobby Ltd., mail order suppliers of craft and hobby products.
West Way House, Transport Avenue, Brentford, Middlesex.

Dulux Paints for supplying paints, stencils, and stippling and sponging kits.
ICI Paints Division, Wexham Road, Slough, Berkshire.

Eurostudio for supplying stencils, stencil blanks, crayons and brushes.
Unit 4, Southdown Industrial Estate, Southdown Road, Harpenden, Hertfordshire.

The Reject Shop for supplying the trolley on page 75.
209 Tottenham Court Road, London W1.

Dylon International Ltd. for supplying fabric pens, batik frames and dye.
Worsley Bridge Road, Lower Sydenham, London SE26.

Tootal Crafts for supplying threads and sewing tape.
56 Oxford Street, Manchester.

Special thanks also go to Katie Scampton and Spomenka Mirkovic for their invaluable help in creating some of the designs featured in this book.